Sister, neither time nor
distance changes the closeness
I feel in my heart when I think
of you... The bond we have
found is everlasting.

Titles by Marci
Published by
Blue Mountain Arts®

Friends Are Forever
A Gift of Inspirational Thoughts
to Thank You for Being
My Friend

10 Simple Things
to Remember
An Inspiring Guide to
Understanding Life

To My Daughter
Love and Encouragement
to Carry with You on Your
Journey Through Life

To My Mother
I Will Always Carry
Your Love in My Heart

To My Sister
A Gift of Love and Inspiration
to Thank You
for Being My Sister

You Are My "Once in a Lifetime"
I Will Always Love You

mija,

I hope you know how crucial you have been to my life. You were there to take care of me when others didn't, you have been there to support me when I was going through a hard time. You have always shown me support that God sent me "you" so that I could be safe. I will never forget & will always be grateful. Thank you & love you

Forever yours,
"Sister" Olga

To
My Sister

A Gift of Love and Inspiration
to Thank you
for Being My Sister

Marci

Blue Mountain Press™
Boulder, Colorado

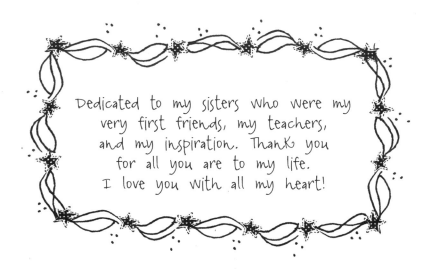

Dedicated to my sisters who were my
very first friends, my teachers,
and my inspiration. Thank you
for all you are to my life.
I love you with all my heart!

Library of Congress Control Number: 2012910292
ISBN: 978-1-59842-688-5

Children of the Inner Light is a registered trademark. Used under license.
Certain trademarks are used under license.

Printed in China.
Fourth Printing: 2013

This book is printed on recycled paper.

This book is printed on paper that has been specially produced to be acid free (neutral pH) and contains no groundwood or unbleached pulp. It conforms with the requirements of the American National Standards Institute, Inc., so as to ensure that this book will last and be enjoyed by future generations.

Blue Mountain Arts, Inc.
P.O. Box 4549, Boulder, Colorado 80306

Contents

6   Sister... I Love You

8   You Understand Me ...as Only
    a Sister Can

10 A Sister's Love Blooms Year After Year

14 You're Not Just My Sister... You're My
    Best Friend

16 I Can't Even Begin to Tell You...
    How Often You're in My Thoughts

18 I Don't Know What I'd Do
    Without You

20 Looking Back... You've Always Been
    There for Me

22 Dear Sister... the Best Times in My
    Life Include You

24 Remember When...

26 The World Needs More People
    ...like You

28 From the Day You Were Born...
    You've Been a Shining Star

30 The joy I feel when I think of...

32 You Have Taught Me So Much

34 You Are Everything a Sister Could
    Be ...and More

36 I Always Know... I Can Count on You

38 I Hope You Know... I'd Do Anything
    for You

40 You Are an Inspiration to Me ...and
    to So Many Others

42 Sister, an Angel Has Blessed My Life
    with You

44 Through Life's Challenges... I'll Be
    Holding Your Hand

46 On the days when things get difficult...

48 When You Need Help... Say
    This Prayer

50 When You Need Encouragement...
    Remember These Things

52 Remember, you are special...

54 Here's Some Wisdom for Your Journey
    as You Follow Life's Path

56 Be Happy, Sister

58 You Deserve the Best!

60 I Asked Your Guardian Angel to
    Bless You

62 Some Things Change with Time...
    Some Things Never Do

64 We share a history...

66 I'm So Glad We Always Have
    Each Other

68 I Couldn't Be More Proud of You

70 May You Be Blessed with These
    Things That Last... Faith, Hope, Love,
    and Friendship

72 May you have peace...

74 Sister, Here's the Thing...

76 No Matter How Long It's Been
    Between Visits... You're Forever
    in My Heart

78 I Smile, Sister... Whenever I Think
    of You

82 Thank You for Everything You Do

84 There Could Never Be... a Better
    Sister Than You

86 If I Were with You Now... Here's
    What I Would Do

88 Sister, Our Bond Is Everlasting

90 You Are My Sister Always... and
    My Friend Forever

92 About Marci

Sister...

I Love You

Our hearts have grown closer with the passing of time. Through the ups and downs of life, we've come to understand what it means to have each other. Sometimes we talk often... sometimes not. It doesn't seem to matter — the feelings of closeness remain with me because I know you are always there. I love you, Sister... What a blessing it is to call you mine!

You Understand Me

...as Only a Sister Can

Having a sister is so much more than being siblings. It is that soul connection that reminds us that our lives were brought together for a reason and that our paths were crossed by God's hand. Some days, you are a friend when I so need one... Some days, you are a mother when my heart needs consoling... But on all days, you are my sister... understanding my heart as only a sister can.

A Sister's Love
Blooms

Sister

Year After Year

A sister's love is a gift that you unwrap a little bit each year.

A sister is a mirror of things to come and a reflection of things gone by.

A sister shows you the road before you and knows the path you've taken.

A sister is the friend who has been there as long as your memories.

A sister is the one you call when you need to talk to someone who knows your heart...

A sister shares life's journey with you, knowing where you come from as only a sister can.

A sister understands what is in your heart as only a sister does.

A sister loves you today and tomorrow as only a sister will.

A sister walks beside you to share each day... stands beside you when you question yourself... and walks in front of you when you've lost your way.

A sister sees your beautiful spirit shining through on good days and bad.

A sister makes life so much better.

We have experienced a lot
together. We have listened
to each other's frustrations,
comforted each other's sorrows,
and given each other hope
that every challenge in life
can be met. We have given
each other support, comfort,
and, most of all, love. I am so
glad that you are my sister.

I Can't Even Begin to Tell You...

How Often You're in My Thoughts

I don't think a day goes by when you are not in my thoughts. I think about all the times you've called me just to talk about our crazy, busy world, and I feel so grateful to have you in my life. I think about how you are always caring... always happy for me... and always wanting the best for my life. I am so proud to say you are my sister.

I Don't Know What I'd Do

Without You

There are times that I wonder what I'd do without you. I know you are always there for me, even if time has gotten away from us and we haven't talked. Your love and devotion stay in my heart, letting me know that no matter what, I can count on you. Thank you for all you are to me... a bright light... an arm around my shoulder... a hug when I need one... and my friend.

Looking Back...

You've Always Been There for Me

It's important to stop once in a while and look back... to see all the steps in our journey and to think about the people who have walked by our sides. As I look back, I realize what an important part of our family, and my life, you have always been. I am thankful to have a sister like you... still there by my side whenever I need you... always wanting the best for me... and always ready to share whatever life brings.

Dear Sister...

the Best Times in My Life Include You

♥

We were friends, you and I, before we knew what friendship was. Growing up and learning about life together, we found a special bond built on the solid ground of family and values and love. Our experiences have brought us to this place where today we can share the precious things in life, support each other through the trials of life, and truly enjoy being together.

♥

♥

Remember When...

Remember when we were young and the summers seemed to last forever?

Remember the trips to the carnival and the smell of popcorn and hot dogs?

Remember the nights when we couldn't sleep and we thought the reprimands we got were hilarious... and we ended up giggling through the night?

I remember all those things... and as I look back, I realize that the simple things... like just being together, laughing till we cry, and sharing the simple pleasures of life... still bring me so much joy. What a gift I have been given to have you as my sister!

The World Needs
More People

...liKe you

Some people change our lives without even realizing the impact they have made just by being themselves. Your special spirit has made such a difference in my life. I am grateful for the way you are always willing to share your time... for always believing in the best in people... for always seeing the bright side of things... for the many kind words you have spoken... for the thoughtful things you have done... and for the way you are always there sharing the special person you are. The world needs more people like you!

From the Day
You Were Born...

You've Been a
Shining Star

You've had a special light around you from the day you were born... It shines brightly and makes you stand out in a crowd. Your heart is always open, ready to share or just listen to those in need. Your arms are always ready with a hug and a reminder that God has a plan. You are a bright light that shines in my life. You are a shining star!

The joy I feel when I think of our childhood memories never diminishes. Growing up is a time when we make so many discoveries. We learn about what we like... what we believe... and who we are. When I look back, I realize that you had such an impact on my life — one you may not have realized.

All Paths Lead to Home

Together we have shared all those things that help forge an everlasting bond — hopes, values, good times and bad. We have learned so much about life through the talks, the laughs, and sometimes the tears. I will always hold these memories in a special place.

You Have Taught Me

So Much

You have taught me that what makes a "family" is not found in a name; it is found in the heart.

You have taught me to face life with courage and acceptance and that everything will work out as it should.

You have taught me that the things that bring lasting happiness are faith, hope, love, and the comfort of family and friends.

You Are Everything a Sister Could Be

...and More

When I want to talk...
you listen. When I am down...
you encourage me. When
I am happy... you share my
joy. When I am sad... your
hug tells me that everything
will be okay. You know my
deepest hopes and share my
greatest dreams.

Our connection has grown through the years as we have shared the triumphs and struggles of life. I know I can always count on you to give me a safe place to reflect on my thoughts and that you will be there to listen with love and encouragement when I need you. The gift you give me with your open arms and open heart is one of the things I am grateful for every day.

I Hope You Know...

I'd Do Anything
for You

No matter what is happening
in your life, remember...
I'm here for you...
I will always love you...
I'll stand by you...
I'll encourage you to remain hopeful
no matter how hard life gets and
until the light is shining again!
I'll remind you to hang in there
because a lot of people love you more
than words can say!

You Are an Inspiration to Me

...and to
So Many Others

Everyone needs someone to look up to... a model of how to find one's calling and follow that dream! You are such an inspiration to so many. You have demonstrated how to move forward in spite of obstacles... how to stay the course when things get tough... and how to keep the things that are really important in life close to the heart. You have shown that with determination, commitment, and a willingness to share, dreams can come true!

Sister,

an Angel Has Blessed My Life With You

The blessings of an angel come in many ways. Sometimes these gifts are right before us, and it is only through time that we realize just how blessed we are. You are always there to share a laugh, and you are always ready to tell me everything will be okay when I'm down. I have come to appreciate these simple blessings. You are an angel in my life.

Through
Life's Challenges...

I'll Be Holding
Your Hand

It seems that life is always ready with a challenge just when we think everything is going along fine. Please know that whatever comes along, I am right by your side... When you are strong, you will have my admiration... When you are weak and afraid, I will hold your spirit in my heart and send you all the prayers and love I have... When you are overwhelmed with choices, I will be there to support the decisions that only you can make... When you have doubts, I will acknowledge them and then relight the candle of hope with you and remind you that God is with you every step of the way.

On the days when things get difficult, remember it is perseverance that will get you through. Give thanks for the talent that has set you on your path... for the inner strength that has helped you navigate the obstacles... and for the faith that has carried you through the most difficult of days.

And don't forget to ask for help
when you most need it. It's easy
to get caught up in whatever is
happening and not realize that
help is always available just for the
asking. That help is called "grace."
It is always abundant... always
accessible... and always exactly
what we need. Remember, grace
is only a prayer away.

This
♥
Way
♥
Home
♥

When You Need Help...

Say This Prayer

Guardian angel, light my way.
Please be with me through
   the day.
Remind me I am in your care,
and should help be needed,
you will be there.

Angels
Are
Everywhere

When You Need
Encouragement...

Remember
These Things

You are stronger than you realize.

Life's inevitable adversities call forth our courage.

You have a lot of wisdom inside you.

God's plan will unfold with perfect timing.

The voice of your soul will lead the way.

A hug from my heart is only a phone call away!

Remember, you are special...
There are talents locked away
inside you just waiting for the
right time to unfold.

Remember to dream... Dreams
are the start of every great
adventure. When you close your
eyes and imagine your "happy
and successful self in the future,"
you are beginning your journey!

If All Else fails,
Pet the Dog

Remember to listen to your heart...
Your heart is where your courage
lies. When you follow your heart,
you may meet challenges, but each
of your steps will be guided.

Remember, "today" is always the
most important day... Enjoy every
moment of it, and may all your
dreams come true!

Here's Some Wisdom for Your Journey

as You Follow Life's Path

No matter where life takes you or what path you choose, you will always meet challenges. That is the way life is. There are no guarantees, and no matter how many things you do right or how many rules you follow, there will always be that fork in the road that makes you choose between this way or that. Whenever you meet this place, keep these things in mind: You are loved... love will sustain you. You are strong... prayer will get you through anything. You are wise... the greatest gift of all lies within you.

Be Happy, Sister

To be happy, keep these ideas close to your heart:

Everyone needs something to do... someone to love... something to hope for.

Happiness sneaks in when you focus attention on something you are good at.

Believe that your daily work, whatever it is, makes a difference.

When you make someone smile, the good feeling will come right back to you.

Be grateful for the little things that are free.

Happiness is only a choice away.

Hope is believing that miracles are possible!

You Deserve

the Best!

May all the good things you have brought to my life be returned to you.

May your steps be guided through all of life's challenges and your heart remember its true calling.

May your future be filled with love and acceptance.

May love warm your heart every day.

I Asked Your
Guardian Angel

to Bless You

I prayed for you today and asked your guardian angel to stay by your side... to bring you inspiration when life gets you down... to fill your heart with determination when life puts obstacles in your path... and to shower you with grace to nurture your spiritual growth as you travel your path through life. I asked your angel to wrap you in God's love every day!

Some Things Change With Time...

Some Things Never Do

The way I feel when I spend time with you is one of those constant good things in my life. There is a sense of feeling understood... there is a sense of feeling loved and supported... and there is a deep sense of gratitude as I realize I have been given the wonderful gift of a kindred spirit. Some things change with time... some things never do. You should know that the one thing that has not changed, and never will, is how much I care about you.

We share a history that lets us understand each other. There is family that gives us a lasting connection of love, and there is a special closeness that has developed between us as we have shared life's journey.

The year passes by so quickly that it's important to stop and remember what life is all about. Our greatest joys are felt with the people we love, and I want to be sure you know that having you as my sister is a gift I treasure always.

I'm So Glad
We Always Have

Each Other

Even though we are different
in a lot of ways, we are alike in
ways that are so important. Our
values, our beliefs, and the things
we hold dear — like family, love,
and faith — create the ties that
bind us. We can turn to each
other in times of need... we
support each other through life's
challenges... and we share all
the little blessings of life. I am
so glad that we have each other.

I Couldn't Be

More Proud of You

You have faced the challenges of life with courage, compassion, and conviction, and I am so proud of you. Thank you for sharing all that makes you special and everything you are with me.

May You Be
Blessed With These
Things That Last...

Faith, Hope, Love,
and Friendship

May you be blessed with all the good things in life... faith, hope, love, and the blessing of good friends. If you have these things, whatever challenges life brings, you will get through. Your faith will light your path... hope will keep you strong... the love you give to others will bring you joy... and your friendships will remind you of what is important in life.

May you have peace... peace in knowing who you are... peace in knowing what you believe in... and peace in the understanding of what is important in life.

May you have joy... joy as
you awaken each day with
gratitude in your heart for
new beginnings... joy when
you surrender to the beauty of
a flower or a baby's smile... and
joy, a hundred times returned,
for each time you've brought
happiness to another's heart.

Sister,

I ♥ you

Here's the Thing...

The most important thing I want
you to know is "I love you." I am
so happy that we have remained
close through the years. Your love
and support are gifts in my life,
and your friendship is something
I can count on. I love you!

No Matter How Long It's Been Between Visits...

You're Forever in My Heart

Each time I see you, all time melts away. Precious moments come flooding back, and I am reminded of all the laughter and joy we have shared through the years. I am so appreciative of those times and of you.

When I think of you, I think, "What could be better than having someone to talk to who already knows all about me and loves me as I am?"

When I think of you, I think,
"What could be more fun than
sharing my joys with someone
who is truly happy for me?"

When I think of you, I think,
"What could be better than a
friendship that has been a part
of my life for as long as we've
been sisters?"

When I think of you, I think, "We're sisters!" and I realize how lucky I am to share this wonderful gift with you.

Thank You for

Everything You Do

It is hard to put into words a "thank you" with enough meaning for all the times you have come through for me... for all the times you have listened instead of telling me what to do... for all the times you have hugged away my troubles... for the laughs over nothing... for the many tears dried. Thank you for it all.

There Could Never Be...

a Better Sister
Than You

If I searched the world, I could never find a better sister. You are a perfect example of sisterly loving and caring and compassion and concern. Just talking to you can make me feel better, and being with you reminds me of the most important things in life. Knowing that I have a sister like you is a gift of family and friendship wrapped up in love!

I'd wrap my arms around you
with all my heart and wish you
the many wonderful things life
can bring... happiness as you start
each day... family all around you...
and lots of friends to hug you back!

Sister,

Our Bond
Is Everlasting

Neither time nor distance changes the closeness I feel in my heart when I think of you. You are such an important part of my life... always ready to be a part of whatever is happening... always open to listening... always there to share a laugh or dry some tears. And I am always so grateful to have you as my sister! The bond we have found is everlasting.

You Are My
Sister Always...

and My
Friend Forever

In childhood we did not understand the gift wrapped up in a greater plan. Time has taught us about the bond of love, and through that love we have chosen friendship. We have learned together, sharing the good times and the bad, and no matter what, there has always been love. You are my sister always, my friend forever.

About Marci

Marci began her career by hand painting floral designs on clothing. No one was more surprised than she was when one day, in a single burst of inspiration and a completely new and different art style, her delightful characters sprang from her pen! "Their wild and crazy hair is a sign of strength," she thought, "and their crooked little smiles are endearing." She quickly identified the charming characters as Mother, Daughter, Sister, Father, Son, Friend, and so on until all the people and places in life were filled. Then, with her own loved ones in mind, she wrote a true and special sentiment to each one. This would be the beginning of a wonderful success story, which today still finds Marci writing each and every one of her verses in this same personal way.

Marci is a self-taught artist who has always enjoyed writing and art. She is thrilled to see how her delightful characters and universal messages of love have touched the hearts and lives of people everywhere. Her distinctive designs can also be found on Blue Mountain Arts greeting cards, calendars, bookmarks, and other gift items.

To learn more about Marci, look for Children of the Inner Light on Facebook or visit her website: WWW.MARCIonline.com.